W9-BIN-562

Climate Change

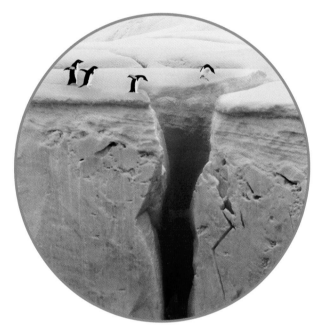

by Helen Orme

Consultant: Terry Jennings, Ph.D.
Educational Consultant

BEARPORT
PUBLISHING

New York, New York

Credits

Cover and Title Page, © Steve Bloom; Credit Page, © Jorge Pedro Barradas de Casais/Shutterstock; 4, © Blaz Kure/Shutterstock; 4–5, © Niclas Albinsson/jupiterimages; 6–7, © Corbis/jupiterimages; 7, © Ximagination/Shutterstock; 8–9, © Mark Smith/Shutterstock; 9, © David Parsons/iStockphoto; 10, © Vera Bogaerts/Shutterstock; 12–13, © Carsten Peter/National Geographic/Getty Images; 13, © John Armstrong-Millar/iStockphoto; 14–15, © Armin Rose/Shutterstock; 15, © Kondrachov Vladimir/Shutterstock; 16–17, © U.S. Army photo by Staff Sgt. Ricky R. Melton; 17, © Wolfgang Amri/Shutterstock; 18–19, © posztos/Shutterstock; 20–21, © Frans Lanting/FLPA; 22–23, © Nick Carver Photography/Shutterstock; 23, Courtesy of the Library of Congress; 24T, © Michael Svoboda/Shutterstock; 24M, © Serghei Starus/Shutterstock; 24B, © Otmar Smit/Shutterstock; 25TL, © Christopher Elwell/Shutterstock; 25TR, © Rob Marmion/Shutterstock; 25B, © Henryk Sadura/Shutterstock; 26, © Peter Zaharov/Shutterstock; 27T, © clearviewstock/Shutterstock; 27B, © Joy Brown/Shutterstock; 28, © Paul Vorwerk/Shutterstock; 29, © Allan Ivy/Alamy; 30 © Kenneth V. Pilon/Shutterstock.

Every effort has been made to trace the copyright holders, and we apologize in advance for any unintentional omissions. We would be pleased to insert the appropriate acknowledgments in any subsequent edition of this publication.

The Earth in Danger series is printed on recycled paper.

Library of Congress Cataloging-in-Publication Data

Orme, Helen.
 Climate change / by Helen Orme.
   p. cm. — (Earth in danger)
 Includes index.
 ISBN-13: 978-1-59716-723-9 (lib. bdg.)
 ISBN-10: 1-59716-723-1 (lib. bdg.)
 1. Climatic changes—Juvenile literature. 2. Global environmental changes—Juvenile literature. 3. Global warming—Juvenile literature. I. Title.

 QC981.8.C5O76 2009
 551.6—dc22

                    2008021020

Contents

What Is Climate Change?

Earth's weather is always changing. It changes from hour to hour, day to day, and season to season. The usual kind of weather that a place experiences year after year, however, is called its **climate**.

For example, about 1.8 million years ago, most of northern North America was covered in ice. This **ice age** climate lasted until about 11,500 years ago. Then the weather slowly became warmer and most of the ice melted.

Earth's climate has changed many times in its history. Today, however, the climate is changing more quickly than in the past. Scientists think this is happening because of the way people live now.

°C °F

50 120
40 100
30 80
20 60
10
    40
0   32
    20
10

From 1905 to 2005, global air temperatures near Earth's surface increased about 1.4°F (.8°C).

How Is the Climate Changing?

Changes in worldwide temperatures that once took thousands of years may now take only hundreds. Scientists know, for example, that increases in air and seawater temperatures that began about 100 years ago have speeded up in the last 50 years.

With rising temperatures, storms such as hurricanes are becoming more frequent and powerful. Also, the **polar ice caps** and **glaciers** are now melting faster than ever. What are people doing to make the climate change more quickly?

According to scientists, in the past 50 years hurricane wind speeds have increased by 50 percent!

The patterns of rainfall are changing around the world. Some places are getting much less rain than usual. Other places are getting much more rain.

Fossil Fuels

People today are using more **fuel**-powered machines than ever before. In the last 50 years, for example, the number of cars, trucks, planes, and motorcycles has greatly increased. People have also built many more factories and power stations. Why is this a problem?

A coal-burning power plant

Most of these vehicles and buildings are powered by burning **fossil fuels**, such as coal, oil, and gasoline. When these fuels are burned, the **carbon** they contain is released into the air as **carbon dioxide** gas. Scientists believe that the more carbon dioxide builds in the air, the warmer the planet will become.

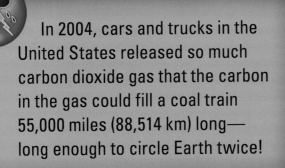

In 2004, cars and trucks in the United States released so much carbon dioxide gas that the carbon in the gas could fill a coal train 55,000 miles (88,514 km) long— long enough to circle Earth twice!

The Greenhouse Effect

How exactly do gases, such as carbon dioxide, cause the planet to become warmer? First, the sun warms Earth's surface. The heat from Earth's surface then warms the layer of gases that surround the planet. These gases are called **atmosphere**.

Some gases in the atmosphere, such as carbon dioxide, trap the sun's heat. These gases are called **greenhouse gases**. They work like the glass in a **greenhouse**, which allows the sun to shine into the building and warm it up. At the same time, the glass keeps most of the warmth from leaving.

A greenhouse

If greenhouse gases didn't trap heat, the world would be too cold for living things. However, if we put more gases, such as carbon dioxide, into the atmosphere, too much heat will be trapped. Then the world will get too warm.

sun

The sun's heat warms Earth.

Some heat coming from the warm Earth goes back into space.

Some heat coming from the warm Earth is trapped in the atmosphere by greenhouse gases.

atmosphere

Earth

Global Warming

The rise in atmospheric temperatures over the past 100 years is due in part to the increased use of fossil fuels. Burning these fuels has released too much carbon dioxide into the air, which may be responsible for **global warming**.

In some places, global warming will make summers much hotter and winters warmer. It may also cause major heat waves. Wind patterns in the atmosphere will also be affected, making storms such as hurricanes and tornadoes more severe. These climate changes will make people's lives much harder.

Hurricanes need warm ocean water to form. As seawater temperatures rise, scientists expect hurricanes to become more powerful and to last longer!

A tornado swirling across a prairie in South Dakota

More rainfall could mean more flooding from hurricanes and other violent storms.

Melting Ice

Heat waves and stronger hurricanes are just some of the possible effects of global warming. A warmer world also means that the snow and ice that stay year-round on tall mountains and in the Arctic and Antarctica will melt! This change is already underway.

In the Arctic, a large area of the ocean called the ice cap stays frozen all year. In winter, the ocean around the ice cap also freezes. Unfortunately, the amount of ocean that freezes is getting smaller and smaller each year.

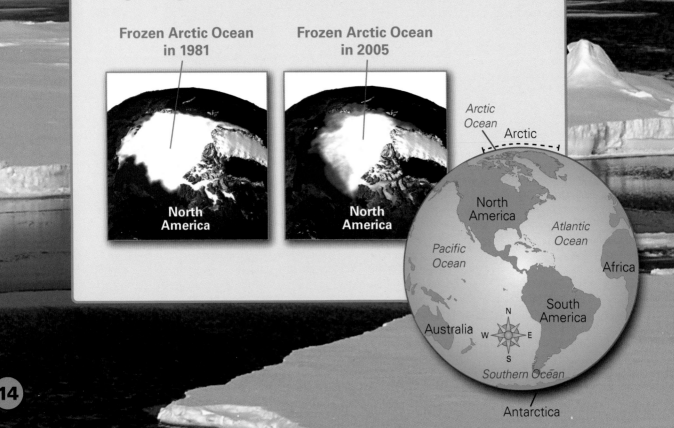

Frozen Arctic Ocean in 1981

North America

Frozen Arctic Ocean in 2005

North America

Arctic Ocean
Arctic
North America
Atlantic Ocean
Pacific Ocean
Africa
South America
Australia
Southern Ocean
Antarctica

In Antarctica, as temperatures rise, giant chunks of ice break off from the huge sheets of ice attached to the **continent**. In 2002, a piece of ice larger than the state of Rhode Island broke off and created thousands of icebergs.

If all the ice and snow just in Antarctica melted, sea levels would rise 200 feet (61 m) worldwide. Disastrous flooding would follow in many places.

Mount Kilimanjaro

Scientists have observed that 90 percent of the world's mountain glaciers are melting—and some are melting quickly! The glaciers on Africa's Mount Kilimanjaro, for example, lost nearly a quarter of their ice between 2000 and 2006.

Rising Sea Levels

Melting ice and snow put more water into the ocean, which makes sea levels rise. Warmer temperatures then heat the water, causing it to **expand**. The warmer water takes up more space than cold water, so sea levels rise even more.

Parts of many low-lying coastal cities, such as New York and London, are in danger of gradually being covered by water as the oceans warm. Very low-lying cities, like New Orleans, may be completely flooded.

In 2005, a huge hurricane—perhaps made more intense by the warmer climate—headed toward New Orleans. As Hurricane Katrina hit, some of the flood walls, or **levees**, which protect parts of the city below sea level, broke. Eighty percent of New Orleans was suddenly underwater! It took 43 days to pump all the water out of the city.

When Hurricane Katrina hit New Orleans in 2005, many of the levees broke and the city was flooded.

The Maldives is a group of islands in the Indian Ocean. Many of the islands are only three feet (1 m) above sea level. Scientists predict that, because of rising sea levels, the islands will be underwater within 100 years!

Droughts and Deserts

Coastal flooding and more intense storms are not the only effects of a warmer climate. Some scientists believe that higher temperatures may lead to severe droughts. These are long periods of time with little or no rainfall. When droughts last for years, bodies of water on land, such as lakes and rivers, dry up. With little rain or other **precipitation**, the land becomes a **desert**.

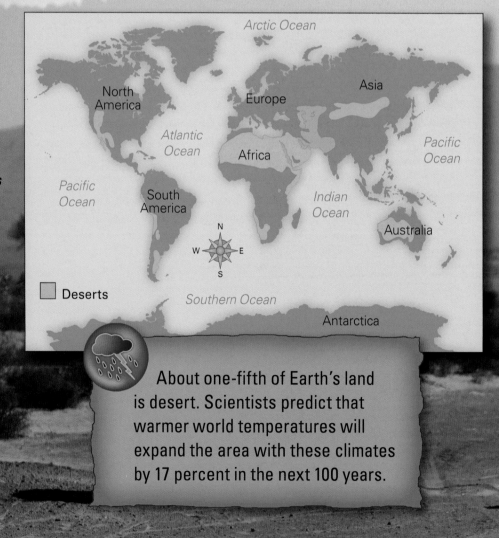

This map shows Earth's major deserts.

About one-fifth of Earth's land is desert. Scientists predict that warmer world temperatures will expand the area with these climates by 17 percent in the next 100 years.

During droughts, soil becomes dry and cracked. Most plants die off. Only a few of them can survive with so little water. Without plants to nourish the soil and hold it in place, the land becomes unusable. Little can grow there, and there is not enough water or plant food to support much animal life.

Animals that graze on dry, damaged land make the plant life disappear even faster.

Rain Forests Versus Greenhouse Gases

The good news is that people can help slow down climate change in many ways. One of the most important things everyone can do is to preserve Earth's forests. How will this help reduce the greenhouse effect?

Trees and other plants absorb carbon dioxide when they make their food. This process slows the buildup of greenhouse gases in the atmosphere.

Earth's **rain forests** contain millions of trees and other plants. In fact, these forests are home to two-thirds of all animal and plant species on Earth. So it's important to protect them. Unfortunately, too many trees in rain forests are being cut down for lumber or to make space for growing crops. If people cut down fewer trees—and plant more instead— then less carbon dioxide will be added to the atmosphere.

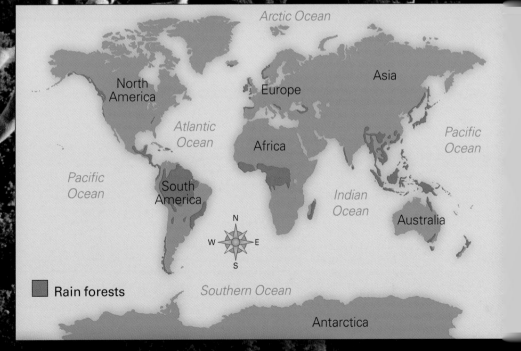

This map shows Earth's major rain forests.

Earth Can Recover

Many scientists believe that human activities are speeding up climate change. Luckily, people can change the way they do things to slow down global warming. They can reduce their use of fossil fuels. They can also learn to use fewer **natural resources**, such as trees, and take better care of the land.

These changes will begin to reduce the amount of greenhouse gases in the atmosphere. Then Earth can begin to recover, just as it does when a small amount of rain brings plants back to drought-damaged soil.

An extreme drought, known as the Dust Bowl, hit America in the 1930s. The soil became dry and powdery. Farmers had cut grasses to plant crops, so there was nothing to hold the soil in place. In 1935, fierce winds picked up tons of this dust and blew it thousands of miles. Better farming practices eventually helped the land recover.

Making Electricity

Today, most electricity is made at power plants that burn fossil fuels, such as coal. Yet there are cleaner ways to make power, such as the methods listed below.

Wind power

The wind turns the blades of a wind **turbine**. This movement then spins a generator that produces electricity.

- Benefit: No greenhouse gases are released.
- Drawback: Wind power works only when the wind is blowing.

Hydroelectric power

Water is stored behind a **dam**. When the water is released, the flowing water turns huge turbine blades. These turn the generators that produce electricity.

- Benefit: No greenhouse gases are produced.
- Drawback: Fast-flowing rivers are needed to turn the blades.
- Drawback: Building dams damages the landscape.

Solar power

Special panels trap the sun's rays and turn this energy into electricity.

- Benefit: No greenhouse gases are released.
- Drawback: Electricity can be made only during the day.

Using Less Electricity

One way to slow down climate change is to use less electrical power. Here are some ways to do this:

- Don't leave the TV on when it's not being watched.

- Turn off the computer when it's not in use. Don't leave it on sleep mode.

- Use low-energy lightbulbs.

- Go solar! If everyone encouraged schools and factories to use solar panels, the amount of electricity needed to power these places could be greatly reduced.

A low-energy lightbulb

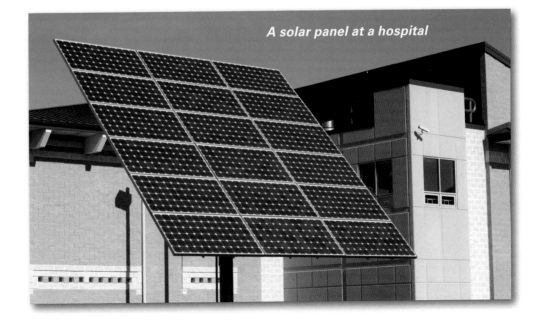

A solar panel at a hospital

Changing Travel Choices

Traveling by car and plane burns fossil fuels. Airplanes produce more carbon dioxide than any other form of transportation. They also release the gas high in the atmosphere, where it can do the most damage. Here are some ways to produce fewer greenhouse gases when traveling:

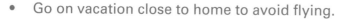

- Travel on foot or by bicycle whenever possible.

- Ride buses and trains. When many people travel together in one vehicle, fewer greenhouse gases are released per person.

- Use a car powered by an electric battery. Some greenhouse gases are produced to generate the electricity for the battery. However, they are still fewer than the amount that a car powered only by gasoline produces.

- Ride in hybrid cars whenever possible. They are powered by electric batteries and gasoline engines. Hybrid cars can switch between the two power sources. They have smaller engines that produce fewer greenhouse gases than regular cars.

- Go on vacation close to home to avoid flying.

Planting Trees

Rain forests are cut down to clear land for roads and villages and for growing crops. Why should people try to cut down fewer trees—and plant more of them instead?

Forests slow down climate change

- Trees soak up carbon dioxide from the atmosphere when they make their food. This helps reduce global warming.

- Trees also fight the damage caused by heavy rains and flooding. Like all plants, their roots help hold the soil in place, so it isn't washed away during floods.

MADE OF
100%
RECYCLED
PAPER

How to reduce tree-cutting

- Recycle paper and buy only recycled paper products. Doing this saves trees from getting cut down and being sent to the paper mill.

- Don't buy items made from rain forest wood. This will discourage manufacturers from using it in their products!

Coping with Climate Change

It won't be possible to stop all the effects caused by warmer temperatures. So people will have to find ways to deal with changes in Earth's climate.

People will need protection from flooding.

- Flood barriers, such as the Thames barrier in London and the improved levees in New Orleans, will help protect whole cities.

People will need to find ways to cope with hot weather.

- Many modern houses have air-conditioning, which uses a lot of electricity. People can get by with less air-conditioning by wearing light, loose-fitting clothing and drinking plenty of water.

- Cover windows with curtains or shades to help keep rooms cool during the heat of the day.

The Thames flood barrier in London, England

How One Country Copes:
"Flood" Case Study, Bangladesh

The problem

- Bangladesh, a country in South Asia, is not very high above sea level. Most of its land lies at the mouths of three large rivers that empty into the sea.

- In 1998, Bangladesh had extreme floods: 1,000 people were killed and 30 million people were left homeless. If storms become even more severe, the country's challenges will increase.

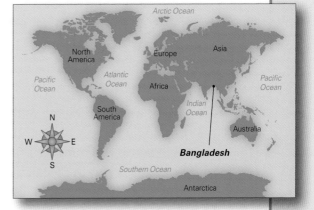

- Some areas of the country are regularly flooded either by the sea or by rivers that overflow after heavy rains.

- The country suffers fierce tropical storms that bring high winds and heavy downpours.

- Many people in Bangladesh are very poor. They may lose everything if their homes are flooded.

What can people do?

- More and more, people in Bangladesh are building homes up on platforms, safe from floodwaters.

- The walls of the houses are made out of bamboo, a kind of fast-growing grass that is inexpensive to replace.

This house is easy for people to rebuild themselves if it is damaged by floods.

How to Help

Everyone needs to get involved to slow down climate change. Here are some things to do:

- Re-use! Don't throw away paper and plastic bags. Use them over and over. This practice will help save natural resources, such as trees and oil, and produce less garbage. It will also save the energy that would have been used to make new products.

- Recycle! It takes lots of energy to make glass and plastic bottles and metal cans from raw materials. Much less energy is needed to make them from recycled containers.

- Learn about the local climate. Keep a climate diary at school. Write down the weather conditions for every day of the school year. Add up the number of sunny, rainy, or snowy days during the year, and put the totals in the diary. Leave the diary for future students to look at. They can then keep their own diary, and compare their numbers with those of the previous years, to see if and how the climate has changed.

- Do an energy check at school. Are lights turned off in rooms that aren't being used? Are computers turned off or left in sleep mode? Are rooms too hot in the winter? Make a list of the places energy is wasted. Write down how it is being wasted and ways to correct the problems.

Learn More Online

To learn more about climate change, visit
www.bearportpublishing.com/EarthinDanger

Glossary

atmosphere (AT-muhss-fihr) the air, or mixture of gases, that surround Earth

carbon (KAR-buhn) the sixth most common element on Earth; found in all plants and animals

carbon dioxide (KAR-buhn dye-OK-side) a gas that is a combination of carbon and oxygen; it is released when things are burned or decay

climate (KLYE-mit) patterns of weather over a long period of time

continent (KON-tuh-nuhnt) one of the world's seven large land masses—Africa, Antarctica, Asia, Australia, Europe, North America, and South America

dam (DAM) a strong wall built across a river or stream to hold back water

desert (DEZ-urt) dry land with few plants and little rainfall; deserts are often covered in sand

emissions (ih-MISH-uhnz) things that are put into the air

expand (ek-SPAND) to take up more space

fossil fuels (FOSS-uhl FYOO-uhlz) fuels such as coal, oil, and gas made from the remains of plants and animals that died millions of years ago

fuel (FYOO-uhl) something that is burned to produce heat or power

glaciers (GLAY-shurz) huge, slow-moving rivers of ice, often about 100 feet (30 m) thick

global warming (GLOHB-uhl WORM-ing) the warming of Earth's air and oceans due to a buildup of greenhouse gases in the atmosphere

greenhouse (GREEN-*houss*) a building, usually with a glass roof and walls, used for growing plants

greenhouse gases (GREEN-*houss* GAS-iz) carbon dioxide, methane, and other gases that trap warm air in the atmosphere

ice age (EYESS AJE) a period of time when massive sheets of ice covered large areas of Earth

levees (LEV-eez) high walls or other barriers designed to protect low-lying areas from flooding

natural resources (NACH-ur-uhl REE-sorss-iz) materials found in nature, such as trees, water, and coal, that are useful to people

polar ice caps (POH-lur EYESS KAPS) large areas of permanently frozen ice in the Arctic Ocean (North Pole) and in Antarctica (South Pole)

precipitation (*pri*-sip-ih-TAY-shuhn) rain, sleet, hail, or snow; any moisture that falls to the ground

rain forests (RAYN FOR-ists) a warm place where many trees grow and lots of rain falls

turbine (TUR-bine) an engine that is powered by wind, water, or steam moving through the blades of a wheel and making it spin

Index

Read More

Cheel, Dr. Richard. *Global Warming Alert!* New York: Crabtree Publishing Company (2007).

David, Laurie, and Cambria Gordon. *The Down-to-Earth Guide to Global Warming.* New York: Orchard Books (2007).

Thornhill, Jan. *This Is My Planet: The Kids' Guide to Global Warming.* Toronto, Canada: Maple Tree Press (2007).